Beyond the Rut

Create a Life Worth Living In Your Faith,
Family, and Career

JERRY DUGAN

DOWNLOAD THE AUDIOBOOK FREE!

READ THIS FIRST

To say thank you for purchasing my book,
I would like to give you the audiobook version 100% FREE!

Why? Am I nuts? Well, that's not important.

What is important is that I know you're more likely to finish this book
if you have the audiobook. It's like a multi-modality learning thing.
You'll hear me reading the book (audio channel) and you'll also read it
yourself (visual channel).

Since I'm the one narrating the book,
it'll be like we're having a conversation, too.

Instead of paying $20 for the audiobook,
I'd like to give it to you for free…

BeyondTheRut.com/audiobook

For more information, email info@beyondtherut.com.

ISBN: (paperback) 979-8-88759-599-3

ISBN: (ebook)979-8-88759-502

DEDICATION

I dedicate this book to the following people who are my "Why" and purpose:

To God

When I made that deal with you in the Kuwaiti desert on March 19, 2003 that if I died you would replace me with a husband who would love and cherish my wife and raise my children as if they were his own, I had no idea that Your plan was for me to be my own replacement. Thank you for the opportunity to become a better man, husband, and father, and to live out the Dugan motto, "By virtue and valor!"

To My Wife

Olivia, if I'm supposed to be the spiritual leader of our home, then I thank you for re-electing me every single day. It's because of your loving heart, cuddles, and a whole lot of forgiving me that I have a family and a place to call home. Thank you for enduring and living life with me. We have been through some thick and thin. I look forward to our empty nest years and living beyond the rut with you. May we be blessed with years of laughs, Disney park trips and other travels, and spoiling grandbabies.

To My Children

Jacob and Emma, I am forever grateful that I got to be a part of your lives as your father. You both know that I rarely had the answers. I am so very proud of where you are taking your lives, and am always humbled and amazed at how mature and grounded you have become. My hope is that you continue to push yourselves out of your comfort zones and live your lives beyond the ruts you will face ahead of you. There's also that hope deep down that you'll one day want to go on a backpacking trip with me, so I'm putting it here in writing to see what happens. Haha!

TABLE OF CONTENTS

Download the Audiobook Free! 2

Chapter 1: Meet AJ 11

Four Years Later 13

The Good News 14

Living Beyond the Rut - You Are Becoming a Part of

Rutter Nation. 15

PART I: RECOGNIZE THE RUT 17

Chapter 2: What Is the Rut? 19

Some of the Lies that Keep You Stuck in a Rut. 20

Two Truths 26

Key Takeaways 30

Chapter 3: You Are Not Alone. 31

Eric Giuliani - From Textbook Salesperson to Travel

Photographer 31

Sara McDaniel - From Materialism and Divorce to

Renovation and Freedom 32

Dustin Heiner - Just-Over-Broke to Earning

over $9,000 a Month and Debt-Free 36

Noble Gibbens – Saving His Mental Health and

Family Through Emotional Intelligence 37

Key Takeaway. 38

Chapter 4: Where Are Your Ruts in Life 39

The Five F's 40

Key Takeaways 42

PART II: UNDERSTAND WHERE YOU WANT TO BE, WHY, AND HOW TO GET THERE. 43

Chapter 5: Play by a New Set of Rules 45

Resolving to Do a New Thing. 46

Key Takeaways 49

Chapter 6: If You Aren't Growing, You're Dying. 51

What Is at Stake in Your Life if Nothing Changes? 51

What Do You Have to Gain if You Do

Make a Change Today?. 52

Key Takeaways 55

Chapter 7: Future Possibilities 57

Look up and Look Forward .57

Jamie Rodriguez - Daring to Dream Then Going for It .60

The Success of Others Is Your Inspiration –

Not a Measure of Failure 61

Seeing Beyond the Rut Also Means Seeing

the Barriers Ahead 65

Key Takeaways 67

Chapter 8: Let It Be Written, Let It Be Done –

Let My People Go 69

The Real Proof of Written Goals. 69

Why Do Written Goals Work for Our Success? 70

Some Tips on How to Have Success When You Write out

Your Goals for the First Time 72

When You Download and Go Through the Measure It to

Make It Model, Go in Sequence 73

Many Others Who Looked Up and Looked Forward . . .74

Key Takeaways 76

PART III: TAKE ACTION OUT OF YOUR RUT........77

Chapter 9: SP Time is Now! 79

Find Your Motivation - Get a Sense of Urgency for Today

. 80

Live Like You're Dying 80

Get Off of Someday Isle 82

If You Don't Have a Game Plan, Get One! 85

Key Takeaways 86

Chapter 10: Out With the Old, In With the New. 87

Who's in Your House?. 87

The 20-Second Rule. 89

The Pomodoro Technique. 92

Where Could AJ Be in the Future? 93

Key Takeaways 95

Part IV: Our Stories Matter, So Tell Your Story
and Change the World 97

Chapter 11: My Beyond the Rut Story 99

A First Line in the Sand 101

My First Rut. 104

Finding My Groove Again .106

My Second Rut and Beyond. 107

Chapter 12: Tell Your Story to Pay It Forward 111

Why Beyond the Rut Exists 112

Join Rutter Nation 113

Notes 115

Resources 117

CHAPTER 1

Meet AJ

AJ was 38 years old and married to his college sweetheart. They had two children. His job was the kind of job many of us envy. That six-figure salary and office with a view of a downtown metropolitan landscape brought him a dream home, two nice new cars, health insurance coverage, and all the security you would want. Life was great looking in from the outside. AJ was living the American dream.

There was a problem for AJ. He was going through the motions of life, checking all the boxes he was told to achieve, but life felt meaningless. What looked like financial freedom and bliss was actually a job jail for him, bound by golden handcuffs.

Dragging himself out of bed was a challenge. Mornings were a reminder that he was more a slave to the goals and expectations of others rather than living out his own dream. That jog he had planned for the morning? Not happening. AJ overslept. It was a long night.

The one-hour commute to the office was slow-going. He would mutter to himself about how he should have left for work sooner, just like every other day. AJ was going to be late for another morning meeting. He dreaded what was on the other side of that drive. It didn't seem to matter because he was stuck in traffic anyway. Equally so, he felt stuck in life, too.

His days were filled with meetings, reports, and answering emails. His boss expected results. There was always more work than time in the day to complete it all. Whatever he accomplished today would be reset overnight, and he'd have to do it all over again. Exhausted and ready for the day to be over signaled the time to return home, often an hour or two after the close of business. It would be another one-hour commute, trapped in traffic, and that's when his mind would check out.

AJ would not remember pulling into the driveway. He barely acknowledged his college sweetheart and wife of thirteen years when he walked through the front door. The children running up to him in excitement were another weight on his heart. He didn't have the energy to play with them. There wasn't even energy to put anything away. Shoes at the door, work bag dropped next to it. There was still one more report to finish or one more email to send, and then he would be done with work for the day. Bringing work home was a regular thing. It made his children frustrated their dad was not ready to play with them. His wife felt like AJ cared more about his job than their marriage, even though that was farthest from the truth. He was expressing his love the way he'd been taught his entire life—provide for your family, and this is what providing looks like.

He got through dinner like a zombie, oblivious to the world around him. The more the frustration in his wife's voice grew throughout the evening, the more he checked out into a safe zone in his mind. Why did his family hate him? He was doing all the right things, right?

Nights eventually became watching sports alone. What he really craved was more connection with his spouse, the freedom to go where he wanted when he wanted, and knowing that his work was leaving a significant legacy. He was pursuing the good life, and life felt far from good. At the end of AJ's day, he would go to bed knowing the rat race would start again in the morning.

Four Years Later

This is where you would expect to read a happy ending for AJ, but that is not the case. Yes, he found a promotion, so bigger job bigger paycheck. That was the big hope to get him out of his rut in life. It changed nothing.

AJ still has the same commute, is more bound to the goals of someone else, and his connection with his family is worse. They are growing without him. The dream he was pursuing on the side? He hung it up entirely. His fitness? It's even worse now. He is heavier than when you first met him, and he's now experiencing breathing issues like sleep apnea. His finances seem worse even though he has a higher-paying job. They racked up more debt, newer cars, and new furniture in a new house.

Even though they can afford vacations on a bigger scale, he is afraid that he can't really take time off from work because a major project will fail. Going on vacation means more stress rather than rest from stress.

If nothing changes, AJ is worried that his life will fall apart in the next few years. Everything from his family life, fitness, and finances are at stake. There is also that nagging feeling that no matter what he does at his job, he's just one skillset, or project, away from being fired or ultimately un-hirable. **Do you find yourself resonating with parts of AJ's story? This doesn't have to be you.**

The Good News

AJ is not real. He is my "Avatar Joe," the person I speak to in every episode of my podcast, Beyond the Rut. AJ is a composite character based on friends, guests, clients, and myself rolled up into one person. While AJ is fiction, the issues he faces and the pain he feels may be very real to you. You may be going through something like AJ. Life is good, but is it really?

Your life is real, and it is happening right now.

The good news is that you are reading this book, and with that, you are making an investment into your future to do something different, something worth living. That will be a future you designed and one that brings you fulfillment, contentment, and impact toward significance.

Living Beyond the Rut - You Are Becoming a Part of Rutter Nation

My podcast, Beyond the Rut, began as a project among three friends having lunch at a deli. We served together as leaders in our church's men's ministry. Each of us has lived our lives on a journey to be the best husband, father, and leader we could be, searching to find success in the areas of our faith, family, fitness, finances, and future.

Beyond the Rut is a podcast that shares encouraging stories of those who felt stuck in a rut somewhere in their lives and now have practical and actionable advice for you. The goal is to encourage you, inspire you, and equip you so that you can make your dreams become a reality without losing your faith, family, or health in the process.

I combined my seven years of stories from Beyond the Rut with nearly two decades of experience leadership development and coaching and serving in men's ministry to put this book together.

You need to know your R.U.T. to get unstuck and live a life that is beyond the rut. That is the journey you are about to take with me by reading this book. You will learn how to (1) RECOGNIZE the rut you are facing, (2) UNDERSTAND where you want to go and how to get there, then (3) TAKE ACTION to build momentum and create a new path into that life worth living.

This book will share with you principles that have helped me transition from facing a life filled with poverty and loneliness to experiencing the following:

- Being married for over two decades and still going.
- Being a present and engaged father for my children.
- Being the first in my family to graduate from college and get a Master's degree.
- From selling plasma to make ends meet to earning a six-figure salary in ten years.
- Being promoted from consultant to manager to director in six years.
- Eliminating consumer debt, car payments, and mortgage by age 45.
- Overall, finding both contentment and a sense of purpose in this life.

I will also share with you why you may feel like you are stuck in a rut even though you've done everything society told you about achieving success. From there, I will help you see a vision beyond your rut and use stories from past guests of Beyond the Rut who are living their dreams outside the confines of their self-made prisons and who are helping others do the same.

Each chapter will end with key takeaways and action items to consider throughout our journey together.

If you're ready, let's proceed to Part 1 of this four-part ride.

PART I

RECOGNIZE THE RUT

"Knowing yourself is the beginning of all wisdom."

- Aristotle

CHAPTER 2

What Is the Rut?

The Rut is a place in life where you are just going through the motions. It does not matter if you are considered successful by others. A nice car, home, a high income, and anything else that comes with the American Dream are not enough to satisfy you. An emptiness permeates throughout your sense of being.

Appearances may look great, but a life in the rut feels like living in a house of cards that can topple down at any moment. Therefore, you have to keep doing what you are doing, even if it costs your dreams, passions, and vision for a better future. You feel trapped but can't place why you feel trapped. At least, not yet.

Maybe financially, you feel the way I once did back in 2005. Having just paid off thousands of dollars in credit card debt over the span of twelve months, I laid in bed the day after Christmas wondering how I was back where I started. Somehow, Christmas surprised the family by showing up in December that year. My wife and I couldn't possibly let the kids miss Christmas.

The thought of scraping by to pay that debt off over another twelve months was like a crushing weight on me. How did a holiday celebrating the birth of my Messiah become a day that was all about the presents? Why did I let my family fall into that trap again? Is this the way life will be until the day I die? What is the point of life if it is all about putting myself into bondage? How did I wind up in the Rat Race after all?! I was trying to avoid this!

Some of the Lies that Keep You Stuck in a Rut

There are a number of lies that you may have internalized, keeping you stuck in a rut. Let us take a look at some of those lies; then, I will discuss truths you can speak into your life and start making your own path out of your rut.

Lie #1 - I'm not good enough or not worthy.

The first lie you may face keeping you in a rut is believing "I am not good enough, or worthy enough, to have the life I dream of living."

Children at a young age feel they can do anything. They just do it with confidence and excitement. "I'm going to be a fireman when I grow up!" or "Look at this drawing I made of you, Dad!"

In adulthood, that shifts in a terrible way. "I could never be a fireman because [insert excuse here]," and "I would draw you a picture, but I'm a terrible artist."

Some of that influence comes from people outside of you whom you've allowed to reinforce any internal doubts you have. There are two types of people who will tell you that you are not worthy.

1. The Drowning Victim

I learned how to swim when I was seven years old. It was a different time back then when I could get on my bicycle, ride a few miles to the community swimming pool, and take swimming lessons offered by American Red Cross certified lifeguards.

There was one lesson from my intermediate swim lessons that stood out to me when we covered a short lesson on rescue swimming. The person who is drowning is desperate and will drown you if you get too close to his or her reach.

The first type of person is like that drowning victim. There is not much going on in their own lives, so they lash out, drowning others so they can stay afloat and breathe just a little longer. The Internet refers to these types as trolls. Some of us can think of bullies or toxic people. Some of us just call this type family like aunts, uncles, cousins, or grandpa.

Those who feel they have nothing going on in their own lives feel, often without realizing it, that they need to speak negatively about your life. You pursuing your dreams, or a life you feel is worth living, represents what they don't have. It is rarely about you and all about them. They're sharing with you what's going on inside their own hearts about themselves.

Your desire to live a better life is a reminder to them they settled for their own ruts. It is easier for them to keep you there on the rutted path with them than to encourage you to make your own path and live the life you feel called to live. Somehow that translates to they have to get out of their own comfort zones and lunge into the unknown with you. They're drowning and attempting to take you down with them.

2. The Hobbit in the Shire

If you have read J.R.R. Tolkien's books *The Hobbit* or *The Lord of the Rings* series, then you may know where I am going with this reference. The Hobbits are a race of people who live in a beautiful meadow. Their homes are cozy, warm, and filled with all kinds of comforts. Their lives are all about leisure, never going on adventures, and never deviating from routine or traditions. The Shire is safe. It's why the adventures of both Bilbo and Frodo Baggins stand out in stark contrast to this life. Each of them had an internal struggle they faced before going on their adventures, and there may have been times when it seemed easier to hang up the adventure and go back to The Shire.

The second type of person trying to hold you back is you. As you compared yourself to others while growing up, as you took on ridicule from schoolmates or parents, you started to wall up your cozy home in your own version of The Shire.

You may have said the following to yourself at some point in your life:

- "I'm not good enough or ready enough to go on an adventure."
- "Who do I think I am? I'm not qualified to write a book, start a business, be a dancer, etc."
- "I'll get started when I get that next promotion."
- "I want to get that college degree, but I'd have to apply to get in first."

Pursuing your dream starts an inside job overcoming the doubts keeping you in your rut. You can do it.

Lie #2 - I don't have enough time.

The second lie you may come across is, "I don't have enough time."

It's important to leverage your time with intentionality because it is the one resource that you cannot replenish. We are all truly on borrowed time. The question is, how will you use that time?

As you read through this manifesto, you will find that time is what you make of it. You may think that you don't have time because of work, perceived obligations, and the need to relax. You may not have time because you have family responsibilities. Whatever the reason is, time is what you make of it.

Business leaders create strategic plans for their companies all the time. These strategic plans identify the core of the company's business and its values then identify key pillars and objectives that align with the mission and vision of the company. These pillars and objectives then allow companies to create guardrails of things they will always do and things they will never do. Steadfast execution of a strategic plan by leadership means that time and resources are used to achieve those desired goals. You can apply this concept of having a strategic plan to your own life.

Does your life have a mission and vision statement? Do you have guardrails on how you will and will not spend your time?

Lie #3 – I can't afford my dream.

Money! The root of all evil, right? (A few of you may have already corrected me in my reference, "The LOVE of money is the root of all evil." This isn't the point.)

Another lie you may tell yourself is you cannot afford to pursue your dreams.

- That tuition is too high.
- I don't earn enough money to do that.
- I can't afford the coaching program that will help me.
- I can't afford the software or equipment that will help me start my business.

Similar to the time shortfall, you can roll up our sleeves and take the time to inventory where your money goes today. That inventory will show you where money is spent well, saved well, invested, and, most importantly, where it is wasted. A budget will give you a map of where your money goes every month.

You may be avoiding this exercise because you lack the courage to face the truth of where you are. Be strong and courageous. You can do this. You only cheat yourself, and maybe your family and the world you want to impact, by not looking at your current state of finances.

Budgeting may feel like it takes away your sense of freedom to spend carefree. That kind of spending may be the only sense of control you feel you have. That's why it's called "Retail Therapy." Unfortunately, that kind of spending just leads to being trapped in the Rat Race, like how I felt back in 2005.

A budget will give you a roadmap on how to best use your money in alignment with your mission, vision, and life's strategic plan. Just like you may want time guardrails, money guardrails will help.

Where your money goes is indeed where your heart's treasure lies. You spend money on what you care about even if you don't realize you care about that thing, whatever that thing may be.

I am 46 years old at the time of writing this manifesto. I draw from *Rich Dad Poor Dad* by Robert Kiyosaki, where rather than saying, "I can't afford that!" I say, "HOW can I afford that?" In other words, what needs to be done, adjusted, or earned, so I can purchase that ticket to a conference that will grow my skills, the new suit I need for that job interview, or upgrade to software or equipment to free up more time for what matters most to me?

I also combine that with the story of Moses from the Holy Bible. Essentially, Moses already had everything he needed to face Pharaoh. You may be faced with telling yourself you cannot afford something, but chances are you already have the money you need. It may be hidden by things like the money spent on lunches at work, the coffee drink you pick up on the way to the office, or the various subscriptions and memberships you pay for but don't actually use.

When you ask yourself, "HOW can I afford something?" you start to break that lie that you cannot afford your dream. You start to find solutions.

We just discussed three common lies that keep us stuck in a rut, plus the truths that counter them. Here are two additional truths about the rut you are traveling.

Two Truths

Ruts are not that deep, yet you may feel like you are trapped and cannot get out. Here are two funny truths about the rut you are in.

The first truth is that you were conditioned to stay there.

Circus elephants are trained at an early age to stay put. Trainers will put a big stake in the ground and tether a heavy chain to the leg of that young elephant so it cannot move. By the time that elephant becomes an adult, it believes that it does not have the power to go beyond the length of that chain. That belief is so strong that its handlers do not really need to drive that stake deeply into the ground because the elephant never realizes it has the power to pull up that stake and enjoy freedom.

Keep in mind that I am speaking metaphorically to make an illustration. I am not calling you a circus animal. Disclaimer: I also do not condone this practice.

You were trained at an early age in your own social bindings. Below are some of those tethers you have been taught early in life and throughout your life. The resistance you meet going through life may have trained you to put a stake in the ground that keeps you in the same place. You walk in circles around that stake, never venturing farther than the rope on your ankles, and eventually, a rut forms in the ground that becomes easy to follow.

In a sense, you are waiting for someone to release you from that stake in the ground when you have the power to remove it.

Go to school. Get good grades. Get a good job.

I had the honor of chatting with a former superintendent of the Corpus Christi Independent School District over a decade ago. Picking up on my interest in history, he shared with me the history of the school bell and the concept of switching classes. Public school is ultimately about teaching and preparing students to function in a country's society. Industrialization was rapidly growing in the United States at the time public schools and compulsory education were becoming commonplace.

Public schools are scheduled and structured in a way to get the most instruction covered in the time available. It was also a conditioning individuals experienced growing up in the public school system to prepare for a career working in a factory where schedules were announced by the blowing of a whistle or the ringing of a bell. Everything from shift change to lunch breaks was communicated with a signal. The school bell ringing signals to students the start of the school day, the switching of classes, recess, lunch, and the end of the day.

Public schools are designed to condition students to think by the hour and an eight-hour workday. It does not matter how quickly or slowly you learn. Everyone spends the same amount of time at the office, I mean, in school! Your high performers do not get to leave early because they got their work completed sooner. In many instances, they are not challenged much further than the status quo. Your low performers do not get to explore topics and subjects that are relevant to their needs. They have to stay put and endure a standardized track of instruction that does not connect. Everyone in the middle is doing just enough to avoid getting placed in detention and get through the day.

Your breaks and lunch periods are structured. Students do not get to run out for coffee, snacks, or lunch when they are hungry. You had to wait for your turn, your shift, to allow you the time to get what you wanted.

Learning becomes something that is not done for its enjoyment. It is done because you want to avoid punishment. Punishment comes in the form of detention, failing grades, and even the stigma of being held back a grade. The United States has become a nation of test-takers. Creativity and the pursuit of happiness are squashed for the pursuit of getting into college to get good grades and get a good job.

The second truth is that your rut is not as deep as it seems.

I like to hike, and some of the trails I frequent are multi-use trails that allow for horses. The heavy weight of those horses, over time, packs a groove into that trail. All the horses and hikers who follow find themselves mindlessly walking through that rut. Sometimes those ruts become two-foot trenches that are a challenge to squeeze through. Most of the time, however, that rut is just a few inches deep.

It's easy to follow the ruts and grooves of life. Everything in nature likes to follow the paths of least resistance. Our behavior is not much different. In fact, we become like that elephant I described earlier. It becomes easier to go with the flow rather than resist just a little to alter our own course.

Whatever rut you face in life, you can climb out of it, and it may be easier than you think if you will add some intentionality to your progress.

The two truths, in summary, are that (1) you were conditioned to stay in your ruts either by personal choice or external influences, and (2) your rut is not as deep as you think.

Key Takeaways

- The Rut is a place in life where you are just going through the motions, and you have given up your freedom for a sense of security and safety.
- The Rut can be where you are pursuing someone else's idea of success, and it is not aligned with who you want to be in your faith, family, fitness, finances, or future.
- Truth #1 – You were conditioned to stay in your rut.
- Truth #2 – Your rut is not as deep or confining as you think it is.

CHAPTER 3

You Are Not Alone

Feeling stuck in a rut is not a unique thing to you. We all face finding ourselves in a rut if we do not pay attention to where we are going. I had the honor to speak to people through my podcast, Beyond the Rut, who found had their ah-ha moment and recognized they were stuck in a rut. Here are their stories to give you a sense of what is possible and begin thinking about what you want for your life.

Eric Giuliani - From Textbook Salesperson to Travel Photographer

Eric Giuliani is the author of *Sky's the Limit,* which chronicles his three-year journey around the world where he traveled by any means with the exception of air travel.

His first job out of college was a sales role with a textbook company. He traveled to multiple cities on the company's dime. Sounds great, right? Maybe not.

Eric began to feel trapped. His travel was based on some-one else's plan. There was never enough time to visit each city. And they weren't big cities, usually small towns without much to offer anyway as far as tourism. Once he was finished in one town, it was time to move on to another.

It seemed glamorous at first, but the hours clocked waiting in airports, driving across stretches of highway to repeat the same sales pitch again and again took its toll. Eric felt like he was trading his soul for a paycheck.

He recognized he was in a rut. Eric wanted to travel and he wanted to exercise his creativity, so he requested a leave of absence with his employer and took a much-needed vacation. Eric's company decided to terminate his employment when he returned from that vacation. Many people would scramble to get themselves plugged back into the Matrix or get back into the rut they were in for the perceived safety and security of it. This was a turning point for Eric. He was not going back into the machine. This was when he decided to pursue his dream of traveling the world and becoming a photographer instead.

Sara McDaniel - From Materialism and Divorce to Renovation and Freedom

Sara found herself divorced from her college sweetheart in a painful way. Reflecting on her life brought a need for change. Life was only lived on the surface level for Sara. Her ex-husband was the "right type," her home was a status symbol, and she had multiple closets filled with clothing she never wore.

She made a decision to live a life that had substance. Deciding not to buy any new clothing for one year was just one of many transformational moments for Sara. Every item of clothing she had never worn was immediately donated to a program like Dress for Success. With her wardrobe pared down to a few outfits for work, fitness, and relaxation, she made that commitment to buy nothing new for a year.

The experience was liberating for her. Sara was no longer bound to a need to buy the latest fashion because of what the marketing said around her. Her beauty was found in a higher power and a higher purpose. She later sold her home and moved to her home state of Louisiana, where she began to renovate the home of her dreams, a metaphor for the reconstruction of her own life into something new.

You deserve it now—so buy it now and pay later … you really pay later.

Marketing is all around you, telling you that you are not good enough. The United States, as well as other First World nations, thrive from consumerism. Those economies only thrive by people buying or consuming things and services each day. Marketing is geared toward compelling us that we need their products and services to be happy.

Car commercials sell us on freedom, power, and manliness if it is a sportscar or luxury car. Consider other commercials we see geared toward men. Whether it is beer, tools, hair replacement, or erectile dysfunction medication, it is all about power. You're not man enough, so buy our stuff so you can be.

Commercials aimed at women typically have the underlying message that you're not pretty enough, young enough, or mother enough. Buy our products, and you will look younger, be prettier, and be a better mom to your children.

If you don't have enough cash to buy it today, you can still buy it today on credit. That's when you're trapped in your 9-to-5 working to pay off that credit card so you can buy more. Since your cash is going into the credit card payments, you're likely using the credit card to make those new purchases, and you're stuck in a rut financially as well as professionally.

"You deserve to have it your way, and you deserve it now." We are sold that bill of goods over common sense. Since you need to have it now, let's talk about financing that product for you. Many consumers see the transaction as being simply an exchange of a good for some money. What was really sold, like in the example of a car or a house, is a loan.

American citizens are under a mountain of debt, $841 billion total across the United States in 2022.[1] That is nearly double what it was just over 20 years ago in 1999. Adults in the U.S. have, on average, about $6,500 in unpaid credit card debt alone. We are not including mortgages or car loans in this. We look like we are thriving on the outside with fancy cars, fancy clothes, and memorable vacations. The underlying truth is we are just one or two paychecks away from complete bankruptcy. Living paycheck-to-paycheck is seen as a norm. Someone like Dave Ramsey saying we should buy our cars in cash rather than a car payment seems crazy to many people. It's almost expected that we will have a car payment today.

Financing cars rather than paying for them with cash is considered normal. Even worse, we know people who purchase a car with a loan, then trade it in a year or two later. These folks drive off the lot with a new car, but that previous note was not paid off, and its remaining balance carries over to the new note. That means the new car was purchased for thousands of dollars more than its fair market value. A few rotations of this later, and someone is now paying close to $800 per month for a car that should not be more than $400 per month. That difference is all the previous notes that were tacked on to the new note. Why? So we could show off to people who are not even our friends that we have a nicer car than they do? You may know someone who finds identity and self-worth in the type of car he or she drives. Sadly, you may even be that person or have been that person.

The point I am making is that financing and debt places you in a position where you have to keep your job. You cannot lose your job because you will lose all those status symbols you accumulated over the years. The loan industry is not friendly to entrepreneurs and business owners like it is to those who earn a paycheck and receive a W-2 form every year. The process is much easier when you're plugged into a 9-to-5 job.

We may dread going in to work every day. We may despise having to go to a job we do not love. We may feel like prison inmates whose schedules are dictated by someone else in power. Accepting debt as a fact of life is accepting that someone else will be in charge of how your life plays out.

These are just three examples of how we have been conditioned in America to be in our ruts, with two examples that it is possible to make a new path and get out of those ruts.

Here are two more Beyond the Rut stories worth sharing from past guests of the podcast, then we will move on.

Dustin Heiner - Just-Over-Broke to Earning over $9,000 a Month and Debt-Free

Dustin Heiner found himself just one paycheck away from being broke while trying to support his family. A real estate course on investing showed him that he could invest a few years of his life in changing the trajectory of his family's life for generations.

The Heiners worked hard to do two things. First, they paid off their consumer debt. Second, they began saving money for investment properties that generated a rental income. Dustin changed his perspective on debt from one of consuming goods and services to leveraging other people's money to make money for his family.

At the time of writing this manifesto, Dustin owns 38 rental homes that bring in over $9,000 a month in income after expenses. In business, you would call that $9,000 "net operating income." Not bad, right? It's all because he changed his mindset on how to use debt. He is no longer a slave to the have-it-now consumer mentality but instead leverages it to buy assets that make money every month. The rental properties owe (or cover) all the debt, not his family.

Noble Gibbens – Saving His Mental Health and Family Through Emotional Intelligence

Noble is a veteran of the United States Army who, as a graduate of West Point and Ranger School, was no stranger to leadership, striving for excellence, and working with teams. Those are two programs in the Army that expect and demand a high level of attention to detail, servant leadership, and a no-quit attitude. The Rangers refer to it as "intestinal fortitude" in their creed.

As Noble transitioned into civilian life, however, he found himself involved with a success cult in a sense, and his need to please people warped his sense of excellence and leadership. There was a toxic culture among the leaders in his company and peer group. It took a toll on his physical and mental health. He also started to bring that intensity and toxicity home. That is, until his wife held a firm boundary that his behavior could in no way be acceptable at home.

He saw that his family was at stake if nothing changed, and he sought out counseling as well as developed his emotional intelligence to better manage himself and his relationships. It was such a powerful impact on his life that he created a business around facilitating workshops and providing coaching on emotional intelligence for teams and leaders. His podcast, EQ Gangster, explores the positive impact of improving your emotional intelligence.

Each of these individuals faced a rut similar to yours and made a decision to make a change happen.

Key Takeaway

Others have faced their ruts and created new paths, and so can you.

CHAPTER 4

Where Are Your Ruts in Life

At Beyond the Rut, we believe there are five circles of our lives that are interconnected for our happiness. We call them the Five F's, and they are the following:

- Faith
- Family
- Fitness
- Finances
- Future

You may have noticed we didn't put "Career" on here. That's partly because career does not start with an "f." There are not many people who say they want to be remembered for how well they utilized the TPS report cover sheets. We also tend to define ourselves by our career progress, yet we do not feel fulfilled. We will share with you where career fits best.

The Five F's

Faith - This is not necessarily limited to religion. Are you living for something greater than yourself? Do you have a sense of calm and connection in your spirit?

Family - The relationships that matter most to us are not the ones we find in an office from 9 a.m. to 5 p.m. Our families should take priority in our lives, yet we come across people all the time who will treat their customers and co-workers better than they treat their own spouses and children. I admit to being this way when I was a real estate agent. It was a gut blow for my wife to have an argument with me only to hear me shut it off instantly to cheerfully greet a customer on the phone. Why couldn't I treat my wife better than I treated my own customers? This was something that had to change immediately, and I'm forever grateful to my wife for pointing this out to me.

Fitness - Life is more enjoyable when we are healthy. Being able to climb stairs, walk for miles, and get up in the morning without a lot of aches and pains brings a certain level of joy to the day. There is freedom in mobility. It's a drag to be sick regularly, especially if those illnesses were preventable with a strong immune system.

Finances - Chasing a high net worth. This is the area men often strive to seek improvement. How do I make more money at my job? How do I get that promotion? Income is great. Having a high income is even greater because while money cannot buy you happiness, it can buy a lot of things that make life easier. Did you know that the subject of many

WHERE ARE YOUR RUTS IN LIFE

marital fights is money? Either there is not enough of it, someone keeps spending too much of it, or the pursuit of it takes someone away from engaging in the family. Having your finances in order will be a rut worth getting out of and staying out of it.

Future - This category is about enriching our own lives for growth. I spend a few hours each morning focused on a goal or goals that propel me forward in my life experiences. Those activities can include podcasting, reading, writing, exercise, journaling, etc. What are you doing to pour new knowledge and skills into your life? Where are you wasting time and energy that distracts you from the life you want to live? In what ways are you stagnant in the other four categories?

Take some time right now to reflect on where your current ruts exist or have a risk of popping up.

Once we recognize our current state and where our ruts exist, we are in a position to make a change for the better.

Are you ready for the next step of making your own path to living beyond the rut?

Need some help thinking this through?

The very first thing you can do is get a notebook or journal and start writing down where you thought your life would be by now in your faith journey, family, fitness, and finances. This was your outlook on future possibilities.

Where you haven't met a goal is likely the result of either (a) that really wasn't your goal to begin with, it was somebody else's goal, or (b) you allowed yourself to become distracted from your goal. Either way, do not kick yourself. This is an inventory to see where you are right now, so you can decide where you want to go from here. We'll discuss drawing a new line in the sand in the next chapter.

Key Takeaways

- Your life is the interconnection of your faith, your family and relationships, your fitness, your finances, and your outlook on future possibility—The Five F's.
- Neglecting one or more of the Five F's can have a negative impact on your life.
- Intentionally living with consideration of all Five F's brings a sense of balance, focus, and perspective.

PART II

UNDERSTAND WHERE YOU WANT TO BE, WHY, AND HOW TO GET THERE

"All you need is the plan, the road map, and the courage to press on to your destination." – Earl Nightingale

CHAPTER 5

Play by a New Set of Rules

World War I is known for its trench warfare, where modern weapons and traditional line-formation warfare collided. Running at each other with rifles and bayonets was futile as machine guns and heavy artillery rained hell on earth. Soldiers hunkered down in trenches for safety. If you were lucky, you survived the onslaught from your enemy. There was a perceived sense of safety inside a trench.

The trenches provided protection from immediate threats but turned out to be death traps. Artillery could bury men alive, and it was only a matter of time before barrages landed in the right place to do so. Nearly 25% of soldiers involved in trench warfare fell ill to diseases like influenza, typhoid, and trench foot due to cramped and wet conditions. Mustard gas could settle in the trenches concentrating the deadliness of chemical weapons.

Life is like that in some ways. You create trenches that protect you from the dangers of the world, such as failure. Movement seems easy and safe from your trenches. In reality, you are just waiting to be buried alive, succumb to illness, or live in fear that either of those will happen.

Maybe your trench is more like a groove in life. You found an easy path and decided to stick to that path, but in time, that groove became your rut. Stay in your rut long enough, and it becomes your trench where death is simply waiting.

Think about a marital relationship. You find yourself in a groove with your partner where you exchanged date nights for watching a movie at home on a Friday night. It was nice, comfortable, and easy, and you both enjoyed it. That becomes the routine every week, and that is where the rut is created. The effort to impress each other and grow closer to each other does not seem needed until one day, you look up at your life partner, and she says, "I don't know you anymore," or "I feel like you don't love me anymore."

"Where did that come from?" you may wonder. It happened gradually over time, then suddenly.

If you become stagnant in your marriage, career, parenting, or personal development, there is no growth. And, if you're not growing in life, you're in the process of dying.

Look around you. Anything that grows naturally in the world is either in a state of growth, a state of decay, or a combination of both. Your life path is no different. Life takes work. Life takes effort. Life is worth it.

Resolving to Do a New Thing

The tide turned in World War I, which transformed a bloody stalemate into an allied victory. It was the result of an infusion of new troops and new perspective. A shift in tactics was introduced by American troops. They saw the insanity of staying trapped in the trenches where death was waiting for them. They saw the greater insanity of running into no-man's-land to be cut down by machine gun and rifle fire while trapped in barbed wire and mud. They strategically looked up and looked around for a better idea.

Problem	Resolve
Soldiers are getting slaughtered in No Man's Land between trenches.	Let's not do that anymore.
The enemy can see us running across the field in the daytime.	Let's attack them at night in smaller groups so they can't see us.
Facing an enemy trench head-on is suicide.	Sneak attacking a trench from the side with a LOT of grenades isn't fair to the enemy.

The United States' expeditionary force applied techniques and tactics they picked up from past wars in the United States. They decided not to play the game anymore that was only serving as a meat grinder for men. "This is the way we've always done it" was not going to cut it any longer.

Instead, they selected small groups to sneak across No Man's Land, the space between opposing trenches, into the darkness of night. Smaller groups sneaking across open ground and using bomb craters for concealment made them nearly impossible to detect. Once they were within range, they would lob grenades into the trenches, blowing up everyone inside and gaining a foothold inside the trench. Inside the enemy trench, the Americans now had the advantage of surprise and overwhelming firepower fighting the enemy one at a time and taking machine guns out of the fight.

Instead of putting themselves out in the open to be cut down by machine guns and rifles, they bypassed the machine guns and rifles and fought in close where those weapons of destruction could not touch them. They bypassed barriers rather than beat their heads against a lethal wall. What their enemy perceived as an advantage was turned into a fatal weakness. They changed the game with a change in mindset that led to a change in behavior.

Life is hard. There are circumstances out there that can be a barrier or the fuel to the life you want to live. You do not need to play a game where the win conditions are stacked against you. The beautiful thing about life is that you can create your own path and rules of success. Someone else's rules for life may work for them, and they can also not be right for you.

It's time to think about looking up and looking forward to creating a new way to play the game of life. That's what we're going to be talking about in this chapter.

Key Takeaways

- Your grooves or perceived safety can become your ruts.
- You can choose to do a new thing where you find the impact you desire while also thriving in your faith and family.

CHAPTER 6

If You Aren't Growing, You're Dying

Contrary to popular belief, it was mystery novelist Rita Mae Brown and not Albert Einstein who said, "Insanity is doing the same thing over and over, expecting different results." Wanting change in your life but making no decision and taking no action to do something differently is essentially insanity.

Every cell in your body is in constant flux. They are either growing and subdividing through a process called mitosis or getting gobbled up by your immune system. Your life's path is somewhat the same. Despite some moments of rest, you are either growing, or you're dying. The world around you continues to change whether you decide to be a part of it or not.

You only have this one life. Do you want to live it well or in a rut of regret?

What Is at Stake in Your Life if Nothing Changes?

This is a question that we all must ask ourselves from time to time. If we do not reflect on where we are headed, we may end up somewhere we never intended to be.

51

For me, I know that if nothing changes, I will never achieve my dreams and goals. I will never be able to look back on my life with pride and satisfaction. This thought is extremely motivating for me to make positive changes in my life.

I urge you to consider what is at stake in your life if nothing changes. What do you want to achieve? What kind of person do you want to be? What will life be like for your future self 20 years from now if you do nothing to change your path today?

Only you can answer these questions, but they are worth taking the time to think about.

What Do You Have to Gain if You Do Make a Change Today?

The possibilities are endless. So ask yourself a slightly different question—what is at stake to gain if you do change your path, get out of your rut, and take a risk to pursue your dreams?

Possibility - Dream - Mindset

What does your ideal life look like? When asked this question, many people may respond with phrases like the following:

- I want to be happy.
- I want to be successful.
- I want to make a difference in the world.

While these are all admirable goals, they are also quite vague. What does it mean to be happy? What is success? How can you make a difference in the world? These are questions that you will need to answer for yourself.

Think about your ideal life and what you need to do to get there. This may require some soul-searching, but it is worth it to figure out what you want out of life. Once you have a better understanding of what you want, you can begin taking steps to make your ideal life a reality.

When asked, "What are your New Year's resolutions?" have you ever given an answer that you knew deep down you had no interest in pursuing? We may say we're going to the gym because we are surrounded by people who are fit, or everyone else around us said it.

If your goals or resolutions are something you said to impress other people, it doesn't really have any meaning to you for real change. That's the theme in this book. It's time to stop chasing someone else's dream and think about what is meaningful for your life.

If you took the time to really say out loud the life you want to live, what would that sound like? What would you say? What is the impossible you want to achieve but always talk yourself out of it? What if that changed, and it started from within your heart and mind?

Carpe Diem - Living Life to the Fullest, a Good Life

It is often said that we should live each day as if it were our last. This is good advice, but it can be difficult to follow. After all, if we truly lived each day as if it were our last, wouldn't we just spend all our time doing things that we enjoy?

While there is nothing wrong with enjoying life, living each day as if it were our last would mean more than just having fun. It would also mean living with a sense of urgency and purpose. We would need to make the most of every moment and not take anything for granted.

Living each day as if it were our last would also mean being bold and taking risks. We would need to seize every opportunity that comes our way. This may mean stepping out of our comfort zones, but it would be worth it if it meant living a life that we were truly proud of.

It would mean doing what matters most in our faith journey, our families, our fitness, our business or work, and so on. It also means that while we do what matters most, we bring our best effort to the table. There is no need to go through life at half or quarter speed.

So the next time you find yourself thinking about how you want to live your life, remember that you only have today. Make the most of it, and do something that matters. Don't wait for tomorrow because tomorrow is never guaranteed. Live like you are dying, and make every day count.

Key Takeaways

- Life is too short to live stuck in a rut, so choose to make the most out of it.
- Consider what is at stake in your life in the areas of your faith, family, fitness, finances, and future success if nothing changes.
- Consider what you have to gain if you make a change. What does life look like in your Five F's if you decided to live like you're dying?

CHAPTER 7

Future Possibilities

Kids are filled with all kinds of possibilities. They believe they can do anything. Like the elephants described in the previous chapter, adults and social pressures are great at teaching the can-do spirit out of your core being. We grow up with limitations placed on us and learn to keep those limitations imposed long after we have gained the freedom to do something about them. Strange, right?

The first thing we need to do so we can see beyond the ruts of our lives is to look up. You're likely hiking along the trail of life worried about the roots and rocks that will trip you. What is the point of going on a great hike if all you see is the dirt beneath your feet?

Look up and Look Forward

I'm an ultralight backpacker. That means I don't put on a heavy, 40-pound base weight backpack before slogging through the woods. Base weight is the weight of the pack minus the weight of water, food, and cooking fuel. My base weight as an ultralight backpacker is less than ten pounds in the Spring and Summer months and around fifteen pounds in the Winter months.

Ultralight backpacking is a mindset shift that goes light, depends on skills over gear, and creates a greater sense of confidence for me as I move faster and farther than I would if I packed a traditional loadout.

On one trip, I had nearly twisted an ankle a few miles into a 28-mile loop. The terrain was rocky, and I was determined not to have to hobble out on a busted leg. My goal was to finish this loop in 24 hours and not become a rescue story for someone else. It was at the end of the day when I realized that I was more focused on not getting hurt that I missed out on a swimming hole, a shaded grove, and more. These were all things other hikers told me about later.

A couple of problems can come out of hiking for miles and miles without looking up and just being stuck in the groove of the trail, a rut in a sense. The first issue can be veering off-course. You may miss that important fork in the trail and wind up somewhere you did not expect. You get lost and either need to figure out by backtracking where you went wrong or re-route your direction to get back on track. That had happened to me a couple of times on this trip as well. It's annoying to have to backtrack, but that is better than dying in the woods, I suppose.

The second is that you can miss the bigger picture. A good hiking trail will have vista views, streams, and wildlife worth seeing for the memories (and survival if we're talking about mountain lions or bears). The whole point of getting out into nature is to slow down and enjoy nature, and we miss it all when we spend the entire time looking down on the trail. I once hiked with someone who kept their eyes on their phone, hoping for a signal.

On the second day, I took a different approach. I spent more time looking up and looking forward with glances down below to make sure my feet were on the right path and avoiding the major obstacles. By looking up and looking forward, I saw a herd of deer that stayed ahead of me for about a mile, I watched the sunrise, and I captured some very beautiful videos and pictures.

Looking down is important from time to time, but it is when we look up during a hike that the world opens up around us. My friends are often jealous of the pictures of deer, hogs, rabbits, and armadillos I've captured. The secret is being able to see them before being seen by them. I'm intentional about looking up and looking forward when I hike. The added benefit of looking up and looking forward more is that I also see potential hazards as well as opportunities much sooner.

The same concept has applied to my own life as well. Looking up at home means seeing your spouse and children in the moment, appreciating their laughter and their troubles, and being there for them much more readily.

Looking up and looking forward at work means taking a step back from the day-to-day grind and spending time thinking through what really matters. You get to collaborate with your team to increase efficiency and effectiveness as you think through the 20 percent of the work that accounts for 80 percent of your results, The Pareto Principle.

Visualization is a form of looking up and looking forward. You are not physically looking at the future of your life. You are, however, looking at where you came from and imagining where that will take you in the future. You get to visualize alternate paths and start making decisions on what direction to take next.

What do you see when you look up and look forward in your life? Where do you want that trail to lead you? What do you want to see and experience along the way? What do you actually see as you look up and look around that is worth appreciating?

You may not have asked yourself these questions before. Well, now is the time to do it. One who waits for perfect conditions achieves nothing.

Jamie Rodriguez - Daring to Dream Then Going for It

Jamie worked for a credit union. Going to work every day and looking up the stairs to the second floor that led to her office was the moment that drained her energy. She knew that for the next eight hours, her life belonged to a financial institution. Her dream to own a company that created inspirational t-shirts would go on hold one more day. Bills needed to be paid.

Something had to change. A short vacation to New York City expanded her scope of vision. Corpus Christi, Texas, was a big city for Jamie. That changed when she saw how much bigger everything was in NYC. It became more apparent when she returned to Corpus Christi. As the plane taxied up to one of the six gates that make up Corpus Christi International Airport, it dawned on her that she did not need to live in her rut any longer. It was time to make the move to pursue her dream. That dream was not going to follow the grain of going to school, getting good grades, and getting a good job. Business owners built NYC, and she would need to become a business owner to make her dream a reality, too.

You can listen to Jamie's story on Beyond the Rut at BeyondTheRut.com/043, where she shares how seeing her hometown from the air compared to seeing the bird's eye view of New York City changed her perception of what can be.

The Success of Others Is Your Inspiration – Not a Measure of Failure

It is easy to fall into the trap of comparison. Comparing your life to someone else's life is comparing yourself to a definition of success that is not your own. Your path may look similar to someone else's, but it will have your own flavor and perspective that makes it uniquely your own as well.

It's a fine line when I share the stories that I have so far. The success stories I have shared with you so far are not to make you feel bad about where you are in your life. Their stories are shared to give you the inspiration to think about what is possible.

When we hear a story of somebody who is doing well, succeeding in the path that they've created in front of them, it gives us an opportunity to learn from that path. Hearing Jamie's story of leaving her day job at a credit union to start a t-shirt fashion business online did not mean that I needed to also quit my job and start a t-shirt business. Her story reminded me that the world is bigger than my town of Corpus Christi, Texas. The Beyond the Rut podcast was thinking small as if we were only allowed to connect with other podcasters locally ... all eight of them. Thinking bigger meant needing to see what else was possible, going to a conference, and also connecting on social media with podcasters whether or not they were in the Christianity or self-help space.

Hearing the stories of Beyond the Rut's guests over the years, plus connecting with podcasters, authors, and entrepreneurs, have grown me in entirely different ways. None of my guests, except for Andy Storch from Own Your Career Own Your Life, work in the corporate learning and development industry. Yet, their stories of success have helped me quadruple my salary and take on two promotions from education consultant to team director. If I choose to continue in this career, I'll likely be a VP of Learning and Development somewhere soon and even a Chief Learning Officer.

I don't say, "Must be nice ____" or some other knock-the-other-person-down comment. That's just loser-talk holding me back. Celebrate their success with them, and draw any lessons that can help you become the better version of yourself that you desire.

Some of the stories we share on the Beyond the Rut podcast may relate to you very directly, such as finding yourself with some kind of paralysis like Peter Hastings or Scott Sunderland, who both found themselves at some level of stress-induced paralysis. They redefined what success meant for them and evaluated how they were spreading their lives too thinly. It was in putting their most important relationships first and aligning their activities to their core values that they saw healing and thriving follow.

You may be like Lee Cockerell, a former Walt Disney World executive who opened Disneyland Paris and later ran Walt Disney World Resorts. Lee grew up in a poor home in Ardmore, Oklahoma. He had a rough childhood while growing up. One thing he had going for him was a hard work ethic and a desire to do better today than he was yesterday. A few years back, Cockerell retired as the senior vice president for the Walt Disney Resorts in Orlando, Florida. This does not mean that you're a success if you run Walt Disney World, and you're not a failure if you don't. This was his journey, not yours. So what?

His illustrious career started from humble beginnings. His success is proof that in the United States of America, we have career, financial, and social mobility. Lee was not handed a great hand at the beginning of his life. His success was the result of knowing he wanted to be better today than he was yesterday by hustling and serving the needs of others.

His applicable lesson for us is, "If you see an opportunity, take it, but make sure that it is aligned with who you are, how you're gifted, and what you really want to do with your life." Pursue excellence to your fullest capability, and you'll see yourself stretch beyond whatever limiting beliefs you may have had before.

You are not a failure because you did not achieve someone else's success. In fact, you are probably feeling stuck in a rut because you are trying to achieve someone else's definition of success.

What would make you a failure is when you have the opportunity in front of you, and you talk yourself out of the very opportunity you've been telling folks that you're seeking! If years from now you're doing exactly the same thing without any growth or leap of faith, I still won't call you a loser or failure, but I will tell you that you wasted those years of opportunity for growth and life-changing experiences.

That, my friends, is a failure, but that failure is not because of what someone else has done to you. It is your response to stories of inspiration and opportunity that makes or breaks your potential for success.

What if I try, but I fail? What if you don't fail? What do you have to gain if you succeed, and how do you mitigate your risk?

Seeing Beyond the Rut Also Means Seeing the Barriers Ahead

A true reconnaissance is looking for both opportunities and hazards.

I served in the United States Army from 1999 to 2003 as a combat medic. My medic training closed out in Camp Bullis with a field training exercise where I performed the role of patrol leader with a squad of Soldier Medics. That meant I planned the route, assigned roles, and ultimately led a mission to secure a hot landing zone, rescue wounded soldiers, and extract everyone to safety.

We had moved approximately two to three miles and were close to our destination when we were faced with a barbed wire fence. Time was running out. The recommendation was to go straight through the fence, but I knew that our gear would get tangled in the wire, and we would become sitting ducks in that delay. That section of fence was out in the open. It would have been the perfect kill zone for the enemy. (We also weren't allowed to cut the wire since it was government property, and it was just a training exercise. I was scolded by the cadre when I busted out my Leatherman multi-tool to cut a hole in the fence.)

I needed a bigger picture to make a better decision. Sitting tight was not an option, and going forward put us at undue risk of dying. I went against the recommendations from the cadre and my team and sent one scout left and one scout to the right to look for opportunities we may have missed. They were given limits to go no further than 500 meters.

65

The scout on the right returned to report he didn't find any breaks in the barbed wire fence. The scout on the left, however, came back and reported there was a gaping hole just 50 meters away from us. We adjusted the patrol, rushed the gap to avoid getting mowed down by possible machine gunners, and arrived on the scene to perform our rescue mission. The operation was a success! Well, except for the guy who fell asleep in the woods pulling security, but that was his learning moment.

Life is a lot like that patrol that turned into a rescue mission. We move forward in life when we are faced with an obstacle or opportunity and plans have to change. Barriers like that barb-wired fence will show up, and we can choose to be stopped by it, slowly go through it, or find new opportunities to go around it and get back on mission.

There are moments when we have all the information we need to move forward, and there are moments when we need to gather more information to make a better decision.

To stay on mission, it's important to put limits on the information gathering. The risk is to stay in perpetual information-gathering mode and never take action. The person waiting for perfect conditions will never get anything done.

A key part of our success and survival on that mission was the soldier "on point" at the front of the patrol spotting all the dangers ahead and relaying them back to me using hand signals. Many of us move forward in life, going through the motions, and don't realize when we are about to hit a wall until it is there. Things gradually build up until, suddenly, they are untenable. My point man saw the obstacle and immediately reported it back to me so that we could tackle the issue. We didn't just look at the ground in front of us. We looked up. We looked forward, and we also looked all around.

Key Takeaways

- Living Beyond the Rut means intentionally looking up and looking forward to see what is ahead of you.
- See the success of others as inspiration for your own success and not as discouragement.
- Looking up also means looking around the obstacles you think are holding you back.

CHAPTER 8

Let It Be Written, Let It Be Done - Let My People Go

If you have watched the Charlton Heston classic movie "The Ten Commandments," then you are familiar with his demand to Pharaoh, "Let my people go!" Each cry to Pharaoh to release the Hebrews from slavery and let them go seek their own lands outside of Egypt was met with Pharaoh declaring an edict to make life worse for the Hebrews.

Once the edict was declared, Yul Brenner, who portrayed the role of Pharaoh in the film, would say this line, "Let it be written. Let it be done." It was my college roommate's favorite line in the entire movie, and he would quote it every time he made a decision. Well, it stuck.

The Real Proof of Written Goals[2]

Gail Matthews and her team of researchers published results from their study on goals in 2007. Participants were divided into five groups. Group 1 only thought about their intentions and did not write down any goals. Groups 2 through 5 had written goals with added layers of accountability for Groups 3 through 5.

All four groups that had written goals performed significantly better than the group that did not. Group 5 performed the best out of all five groups.

The ingredients for Group 5's success were attributed to the following:

- Clear and written goals
- A commitment to take action
- Shared goals with a friend or coach (an accountability partner)
- Requirement to provide a progress report to their accountability partner

So, let it be written! Let it be done!

Why Do Written Goals Work for Our Success?

There are a few reasons why written goals bring so much value to our success.

First, they keep our perspective future-focused. This means that when we read a goal we have written, we are reading our own voice, creating a future in our minds. A goal does not make excuses for your current situation or for your past.

Second, a written goal makes your thoughts or ideas tangible, so something that was abstract and nebulous inside your head has now been created because you've written it down. That's the power of having your goals written.

Until you've written them out on paper, your goals are really just dreams without a deadline and without life.

Writing goals gives your dreams structure and reality. Just as we are spiritual beings placed in a fleshly body, your dreams for the future do not have a body until you've written them down on paper.

Third, your written goals give you a destination, and a map, for your new path. Have you ever gone through the woods or on a long road trip without a map? It's not a good idea. Unless it is a route you've taken every single day, going into the wilderness without a map and a compass is a great way to become a news headline across the world. Your written goals now give you a path, milestones, or waypoints, and you're now able to track your progress toward a new life beyond your rut.

These are three reasons why written goals work for your success. They give a sense of the future, they become a reality the moment you write them out, and they give you waypoints to a new destination.

I invite you to download a free tool called Measure It to Make It from the Beyond the Rut website at BeyondTheRut.com/goals. You'll have a model that guides you through identifying your core values, the things in life that matter most to you, and the life YOU dream of living beyond your rut.

Measure It to Make It will take you through a life where money was no object and time was no object as a starting point to your goals. You'll take a look at what you feel success will look like in your faith, family, fitness, finances, and outlook on future possibilities. Let Measure It to Make It help you turn your dreams into reality.

71

Some Tips on How to Have Success When You Write out Your Goals for the First Time

- Choose a quiet place where you can be alone—you need to be able to think without distraction.
- Give yourself time—I spend at least half to a full day on this exercise to give it the seriousness it deserves. We're talking about your life and your future and maybe the generations that follow you.
- Slow down to go fast—it seems counter-intuitive, but the Navy SEALs, when doing close-quarters battle, follow the maxim that "Slow is smooth. Smooth is fast. Fast is lethal." You will be more thorough, efficient, and effective when you slow down to think through each step of the process.
- Review what you've written—is it really coming from you or something you feel needs to be in your goals because it's expected of you or sounds cool to say to others? Screw that! This is your life, and those other people aren't paying your bills!

The biggest mistake I see men make, and this goes back to when we were young teenagers, is we spend a lot of time conforming and trying to impress other dudes. Why? Most men are not trying to start a family with another man, but we spend a lot of time trying to impress other men. In what ways would your life change if that did not matter anymore? In what ways would your life seem more authentic?

This entire book is about challenging you to get past that obsession to impress other men. You are here to live out your life and your dreams, not what someone else says success is.

When You Download and Go Through the Measure It to Make It Model, Go in Sequence

Written goals should be both outcome-based as well as activity-based. Outcome-based goals are what you want at the end of a time period (like your life, ten years, five years, this year, etc.) Activity-based goals are the daily, weekly, and monthly actions you commit to completing that will build momentum and deliver the outcome-based goals you've declared.

Examples of Outcome-Based Goals
- Write a book by the end of the year.
- Graduate with a college-level degree.
- Compete on a television game or competition show.

Examples of Activity-Based Goals
- Write 500 words a day.
- Apply to five universities or colleges that meet my criteria.
- Create and submit demo reels for the shows you want to be on.

Many Others Who Looked Up and Looked Forward

The episodes of the Beyond the Rut podcast are filled with people who found themselves in a rut, then looked up and looked forward to a new life.

Michael Lacey was one of those many stories. He had just married the woman of his dreams, and it was on his honeymoon that he looked up and realized with a sinking feeling that they were over $61,000 in debt to start their marriage. He was supposed to be celebrating a new adventure with his wife, and instead, he felt the unbearable burden of debt on him.

This realization led to a tough, honest, and loving discussion with his newlywed sweetheart. Because he was able to look forward with his spouse, they put together a plan of action. They worked hard at their plan and paid off that debt. With their debt gone, life got better because they increased their monthly cash flow.

The Laceys now teach couples how to prioritize their expenses, increase their income, and see in the long run how life will be better without the strain of debt. No debt means freedom.

I cannot take credit for the Mindset Answer Man, **Cliff Ravenscraft**. He can, in some ways, take credit for me. I've been following Cliff long before I got into podcasting when he was known as the Podcast Answer Man. His work for the past decade or more has been about looking up and looking forward and helping others do the same.

Cliff was working in insurance. It paid well, but it was not fulfilling for him. He felt stuck. He looked up and realized that his passion for podcasting and sharing insights about his favorite things could actually earn an income. Cliff was able to replace what he was earning as an insurance salesman.

He has hit other ruts in his life since, and having a look-forward mentality has allowed him to work out of every single one. For example, Cliff's health was at risk. He shared his weight-loss journey with his audience, and they loved it. His self-confidence grew, and his audience enjoyed it. He was providing a value bigger than coaching people on how to start a podcast.

People were now following him for a life change. Seeing that his earning potential was limited as a podcast coach, he shifted gears and runs mastermind groups where he brings together high-performing individuals who seek to do better than they did yesterday.

By looking up and realizing that he was stuck in his own rut, Cliff saw that he had created his own limitations. By looking forward, Cliff realized he could surpass his current level of success. He now helps others shift their mindsets as well.

In the last chapter, we talked about looking up and realizing where you are now may be a rut. It may be someplace where you got stuck without realizing it until you looked up.

This chapter has been about how you can look forward as far as the path can see, and you can also look beyond that using your imagination. By looking forward, you are now able to turn your dreams into reality with written goals.

Let's now take a look at how you create that map to steer you into the future to guide you forward … here we go!

Key Takeaways

- Written goals will improve your chances for success compared to not having written goals.
- The best system with written goals seems to include the following elements: written goals, commitment to action, sharing those goals with an accountability partner, and providing that partner with weekly progress reports.
- Download a free tool to help you write out your goals called Measure It to Make It at BeyondTheRut.com/goals

PART III

TAKE ACTION OUT OF YOUR RUT

"You miss 100% of the shots you don't take."

– Wayne Gretzky

CHAPTER 9

SP Time is Now!

When I was a medic in the Army and on deployment to Kosovo in 2000, we went on regular patrols into the neighborhoods along the streets and highways. We would be briefed by the patrol leader before every patrol, and he would tell us, "SP time is _____." I'd ask the other patrol members what "SP time" meant, and they would tell me just to be there fifteen minutes prior to that time, ready to go.

I learned later on "SP Time" meant "Start of Patrol." In other words, the mission started at that time, and you needed to be ready to go.

Up to this point, you have realized a rut you face and thought about what life will look like beyond that rut. Maybe you even took the time to write out a vision, life plan, and goals to get you to that life.

If that is you, SP time is now.

That does not mean tomorrow, next week, or when that raise comes in. It does not mean waiting for perfect conditions, either. Anyone who waits for perfect conditions is doomed to never start at all.

In this section of the book, we'll talk about strategies to help you get started, take action, and not only get out of your rut but live beyond it.

Find Your Motivation - Get a Sense of Urgency for Today

I don't know about you, but I have found that my most productive days in a 9-to-5 job have been the day before leaving for vacation.

There is a sense of clarity and prioritization that hits me when I have only eight working hours to get all my work in order or else face a wasted vacation where I'm doing as much work off the clock as on the clock.

In those eight hours, you cancel meetings that have little impact, delegate work that can be done by others (and probably should), and eliminate tasks that don't provide much value to the bottom line. You carry out tasks with a focus and fervor like never before. Stuff is getting done because you're getting out of there!

It's when we feel like there's no end in sight that we drag out our work, stay late, and mill around without much impact in the day.

Live Like You're Dying

In 2021, I interviewed a man named Ron Worley II. His youth was spent consuming drugs or at least being drunk through most days. Worley's lifestyle and decisions took advantage of his friends and family. He had a rough life, and as he got older, Ron realized that he was wasting his life. He began to live intentionally, shaping his life around core values. Living by a code he created with the help of a coach, which he calls the Worley Way, helped him renew his life and gave himself direction and guardrails to stay on the path he created. You can read about it in his book *Ditches to Riches: How to Survive Your Effed-up Life and Create a Kick-ass Business*.

That alone is a great Beyond the Rut story, right? Ron's story didn't end with overcoming alcohol and drug abuse to become a successful businessman and focus on his family.

Some years ago, while he was conducting a keynote with an audience of police officers, he felt light-headed. After cracking a few jokes about it, he collapsed and passed out. It was a good thing that he was in a room full of first responders because they snapped into action and rushed him to the nearest hospital.

Doctors and trauma staff were able to bring him back to life and on the road to physical recovery.

The tests came in, and Ron met with his doctor to talk about what was ahead for him. That's when the doctor told him the grim prognosis. Ron had survived the mother of all heart attacks. It was the kind where most die in that moment. He was one of the miraculous few to live.

However, of those who survive, more than half are dead within six months. Half of those who remain after six months are dead within that year. Overall, nearly all survivors are dead within five years. That was the news of recovery shared with Ron in that visit, a life expectancy of five years or less.

What would you do with less than five years left to live?

Your mindset is at a turning point. On the one hand, you can give up. What's the point of it all? Host that pity party where you're the only guest.

On the other hand, you can be like Ron Worley II. He decided to double down on life. Ron chose to live like he was dying, staying true to The Worley Way values, and knocking out items on his bucket list like there was no tomorrow.

"Live like you're dying!" became his daily mantra.

At the time Ron was interviewed on Beyond the Rut, he was at the end of the five-year mark. At the time of this book coming out, he is creeping up on the seven-year mark.

Worley is living like he's on borrowed time. He wanted to publish a book. *Ditches to Riches* was self-published in 2021 with a podcast tour. That's how I met him. He wanted to become a public speaker, and his book was the gateway to that. He even wanted to be in a movie, and he landed a very small speaking part in an animated feature. You won't find him on IMDB, but you will see a Ron Worley happy to have checked something off his bucket list.

Ron's life is fuller today because he lives like there is no tomorrow while building for a better tomorrow.

Get Off of Someday Isle

Each moment is precious and cannot be relived. The saying YOLO, you only live once, is often an excuse to indulge in passions to ruin relationships or do something dumb. What if you use that same phrase to make a difference in the world?

This does not mean you must give up all your material possessions and live like Mother Teresa. It does mean live your best life today, right now.

Maybe there's a place where you want to travel. You've probably been an AJ telling yourself all this time, "I'd love to travel to this place, but I just cannot afford it, or I have this big project due at work."

I say follow the advice of Robert Kiyosaki, author of *Rich Dad Poor Dad*, and ask yourself, "How can I afford this trip?" Add to this question, "How can I make this trip happen as soon as possible? When would that be?" When you start asking yourself that type of question, you're now looking for solutions. You're now looking for a way to live like you're dying.

You're acquiring money not just for the sake of acquiring money but to live life with purpose. Perhaps you want to give a certain amount to charity. You can do that now with what you were earning today. When you live like you're dying, there is no tomorrow where your destination is "Someday Isle" (as in "Someday I'll"). Be a giver, a philanthropist, now!

Take control of your finances. Live below your means and use your money to make the change you want to see in the world.

It may mean reframing your perception of what money is. Many of us are taught your value is in your net worth. Oh, that is simply not true. Your value is in being a unique creation in this world with the power, talent, and strength to make a difference. You can live your life in a way where you find enjoyment, pleasure, and relationships and make a difference that matters to others. And we're not just talking about for yourself and for the current generation. You can make a difference that impacts future generations.

Some of the cool things from Ron's story that I think really stand out to me are from his bucket list. There are some fun things he just wanted to do, and he's out there doing it. He wanted to be in a movie, and so he's a voice-over in a cartoon for kids—check the box. He wanted to write a book and did not have the time to go the traditional route, so he self-published one. It's still out there, though. It's a nice book that may not be your next New York Times bestseller, but that book is live. I read it, and it made an impact on my life. It reminded me that we should live our lives based on our core values of who we are. We should have a creed for our lives and live true to it because that is what people see. Do your actions match what you say you're about?

I chose at a young age to live by the Dugan motto, VIRTUE ET VALORE, meaning "by virtue and valor."[3] To me that means holding myself to a high standard with values that treat others with respect for their dignity and having the courage to do so.

Live your life by a code. Live your life by a set of core values that are non-negotiable. Do the hard right that aligns with who you are, who you say you are, and what your core values are all about. Our values are going to be different from one person to the next. Some people are going to value family. Some people are going to value public service. Some are going to value both. There's no right or wrong answer as long as you are not impeding on the right values of others. Even better, boost the rights and values of others, and you will find yourself going far. It's just like what Jim Rohn said in his book, *My Philosophy for Successful Living*, "If you help enough people get what they want, you can have everything you want."

If You Don't Have a Game Plan, Get One!

Real estate broker Joe Niego said from the stage of a real estate sales conference I attended in 2006, "Many people aim at nothing and hit it with amazing accuracy."

Have you taken the time to write out what a life well-lived looks like for you?

I mentioned in Part 2 how important it is to have a written plan of what you want to achieve in life. A written vision for your life, a "Why" statement, and specific goals are your roadmap to the life you want to live Beyond the Rut.

You can attempt to trust the GPS someone else set for you and take all the re-routes that the app would want you to take in life, or you can go a little old school by mapping out on paper what your journey and destination will look like.

If you need some help creating that vision and an initial set of goals, download this free workbook to guide you through the process at BeyondTheRut.com/goals. The workbook is titled "Measure It to Make It" because you need to be able to measure your results to know if you're on the right track, falling behind, or ahead of schedule. How will you know that you have succeeded in a goal? You have to measure something. Feelings are too subjective and nebulous to be effective tools in showing your progress to yourself.

How do runners know they had a good run? They measure a combination of data points like distance, heart rate, pace, etc. How do project managers know they were successful and can justify the invoice they give to a client? They have clearly defined deliverables and milestones.

Why is it that this concept of measuring outcomes can work for your job or your fitness but somehow cannot be applied to every area of your life? It's ridiculous to hold yourself back from the success you want to have because you think you're too cool for written goals.

SP Time is NOW. Take a break, download Measure It to Make It, and use a few hours to map out what life looks like for you down the road. Don't forget to come back and finish reading this book.

Key Takeaways

- Your best time to get started is now rather than when conditions are perfect.
- Knowing your "why" and living like you're dying gives you a sense of urgency to get things done for the life you want to live.
- If you don't have a game plan for life, now is the time to create one. Download Measure It to Make It, a free tool to help you create a life plan and goals with a focus on the Five F's, BeyondTheRut.com/goals.

CHAPTER 10

Out With the Old, In With the New

If you want to end a habit, you need to replace it with a new one. In this chapter, we will cover why this is so and some techniques that will help you stay on course toward the life you dream of living.

Who's in Your House?

There's a Christian Bible story about a house that had been occupied by a demon. The homeowner basically evicts the demon. Good riddance! That should be the end of it. The homeowner is now free of that demon causing trouble in the home.

Nothing was done by the homeowner to refill that home's empty space with something good and godly. One day, that evicted demon was strolling along and saw the same house. It was still vacant from when it had been evicted, so it returned to the empty space. Not only did that demon move back into its old haunt, but it also brought along other demons, making it even harder for the homeowner to reclaim his home.

There may be some habits or limiting beliefs holding you back from the life you want to live. Those are the demons you may have decided to evict from your life. There is a second step that is more critical than the first, and that is to replace your old habits and your old way of thinking with something new that will support the growth you want to achieve. This is necessary so that your old ways do not return to put you back where you started.

Your roadmap to a life beyond the rut should include identifying what you will stop doing and what you will start doing to replace the old.

Charles Duhigg describes in his book, *The Power of Habit*, that our habits are initiated by some kind of trigger moment. As you identify your habits and limiting beliefs that need to stop, take the time to learn what the triggers are for those habits and beliefs. You may not be able to change the triggers, but you can change your response to those triggers.

For example, if you have a habit of hitting the snooze button too many times in the morning and, as a result, find yourself rushing to get to work while also missing out on the opportunity to spend some morning time on yourself, then some things to consider would include the following:

- The alarm is your trigger, and the current habit is hitting the snooze bar too many times.
- Move your alarm clock to the other side of the room.
- Place a new secondary trigger next to your alarm clock, such as exercise clothes, a book to read, etc. The new trigger replaces what you used to do—going back to sleep.

Your original trigger is the same—the alarm clock. The environment around that alarm clock has changed to support new behaviors.

As you grow and make a new path out of the rut you are in today, you may find yourself faced with another rut in the future. That's okay, and after talking with over 300 guests on Beyond the Rut, I have learned this is normal. You may identify new limiting habits and limiting beliefs that have formed over time. The idea is that as time goes on, you get better at recognizing your new ruts, or threats of ruts, and make a habit of getting out of your comfort zones and limitations.

The 20-Second Rule

What is the best way to stop an old habit and start a new one? Make it harder to do the old thing and easier to do the new when a certain habit trigger comes around.

Shawn Achor, the author of *The Happiness Advantage* and positive psychologist, shares a practice called the 20-Second Rule. The idea is based on the notion that humans are more likely to do something if it is easy to do in a short period of time. Conversely, we are also less likely to do something if it takes too much effort or more than 20 seconds to get started. Think about a web page that takes too long to load or more than two to three clicks before you get to the resource you wanted. You're likely to bounce to something else, right?

The example that Achor shared in his book was his desire to reduce the amount of television at home to almost nothing and read more non-fiction books. It was easy for him to watch television and fall into a time-suck situation. The remote for the TV was right there on the coffee table within arm's reach, and it took no more than three seconds to have the TV powered on and begin flipping channels for something to watch. Simply putting the remote control into another room was not enough. Getting rid of the television and cable service also was not an option for him. At least, it was not an option he desired. Entertainment has its use and value, too, after all.

In the end, Achor put the remote control for the television as far as he could from the television itself. He then took the batteries out of the remote control and placed those in another room. He and his family still had the freedom to watch television whenever they wanted; however, it took too much effort to make it worthwhile. Instead, he would read one of the non-fiction books he had placed throughout the house. The end result was the reading habit he desired by making access to television harder. He also created the time he needed to write *The Happiness Advantage*!

You don't have to go to an extreme Spartan lifestyle with few comforts; just set up your environment at home and work to maximize access to what you want to achieve and reduce access to the things that are fun but not as productive.

The one device I rely on the most is both a blessing and a curse—my smartphone. Having information within a few taps on a glass screen is amazing! It's the kind of world I dreamed of having when I was a kid growing up and watching the TV show "Quantum Leap" about a time traveler named Sam Beckett. Sam was able to succeed in leaping from one time to another because of the help he got from his friend, Al, who gave Sam real-time updates because of a hand-held device that fed him information on Sam's situation. I dreamt of being able to have that kind of power in my hand, and I do now!

The problem is that it's also a gateway for all kinds of distractions for me. That mobile device has my podcast player on it, games, email, text messages, social media, and a whole Pandora's box of entertainment and education that can take a lifelong learner with ADHD-like tendencies down a rabbit hole for hours.

I apply the 20-Second Rule when it comes time to work on specific projects like writing this book. While in my podcast studio/home office, my phone is powered down and often not in the room with me. That way, it would take me roughly 20 seconds or more to leave the room, power my phone back on, and open the app I want to be distracted by. I also had to retrain my mindset that I was not important enough to truly require being plugged in 24 hours a day, seven days a week. No one in this world depends on me for national security and life-saving decisions.

What are some things in your life where you'd like to apply the 20-Second Rule?

The point here is not to create undue hardship on yourself for the sake of creating hardship. That sucks. Who really wants to live like that? The real point is about coming across a stimulus or trigger that leads you to do a habit you want to stop doing, making it harder to start that behavior while making it easier to do the habit you want to do instead. You're leveraging a process that is already ingrained in your brain to do a new thing.

The Pomodoro Technique

The Pomodoro Technique is more of a productivity process for getting things done when you're tempted to let distractions and urgent matters hijack your day.

The method was created by entrepreneur and developer Francesco Cirillo in the early 1990s and is where you conduct your work in focused 25-minute intervals on one specific task at a time. The technique was named after the tomato-shaped Pomodoro timer he used to track his intervals. After each 25-minute period, you'd take a 5-minute break. After every four Pomodoro periods, you would take a 15-to-20-minute break.

Unlike the 20-Second Rule, where you are leveraging triggers that already exist with current habits, The Pomodoro Technique is helpful when creating intentional time for a new thing. The 20-Second Rule can work in tandem with this technique. Pomodoro is about creating the time and space you need to get things done for the future you want to create.

What can you use as a timer for your own practice of The Pomodoro Technique?

Where Could AJ Be in the Future?

At the beginning of this book, you read a story about AJ, the character that guides what is covered on the Beyond the Rut podcast. It's his story, the stories of others who have overcome their own ruts, and your stories that made us come together.

Beyond the Rut is about helping people who experience that defeated sense of feeling stuck like AJ imagine a future. We first help you have your "Ah-ha" moment where you realize there is a rut and something needs to change for you. We then help you think about possibilities through the stories of others. Sometimes, it helps to have a concrete example to begin thinking about your own version of a life well-lived. You then get equipped with advice that you can apply to your life starting today.

I like to think that AJ, just like you and me, hit that low point where he asked himself, "Is this all there is?" and decided, "There is so much more to be experienced!" Here is what I imagined happened for AJ and what I imagine could happen for you as well.

AJ decides that he needs to grow himself for the life he wants to have and not the life he currently has. He realizes that he is already commuting two hours a day, five days a week, and that gives him 20 hours of opportunity. He swaps out his current listening, which could be music or political talk radio, for something that will grow him.

Podcasts like Beyond the Rut or non-fiction audiobooks fill the air now. He finds himself coming to work with new ideas and approaches to solving problems. The more he listens, the more he grows, and he starts to get ideas for the bigger picture. AJ starts to imagine what life would be like if he lived the life he wanted to live. He dedicates a day to taking stock of his life today. What are all the things he has accomplished to this point? What is he most grateful for? What gifts, talents, and strengths does he possess? He also takes stock of where he feels stuck and why.

AJ sees where he is today and begins to write down what he imagines a life well-lived will be for him. He focuses on the areas of his faith journey or spirituality, his family and relationships, his fitness, and his finances, and this is mapping out future possibilities. He decides what matters most to him based on his desires, his values, and his strengths. AJ has planned for the future before, but this is the first time he's doing it for himself.

This is his plan for a future and a life well-lived. It isn't his parents' vision for him, or what his supervisor wants at work, or what some men's magazine manufactured so they could sell him on products that increase their advertising revenue. He has removed the worry of what the neighbors think. They aren't the ones paying his bills, and they aren't his family.

Everything is written down because AJ knows that once he writes down his thoughts, they become tangible creations. What AJ has created is a life vision that is aligned with his core values and includes his dream list of what he wants to accomplish. He finds fulfillment because there is also an added element of how he wants to help others through his new life.

He begins to plan out his daily routines to make sure that what matters most is what gets priority. He has created time for personal development, time with his family, and a set of rules or guardrails to help him decide how to best use his time. AJ's excited now that when he gets home, he is going to engage with his children, and he'll say hello to his partner because he knows they are the reason why he does what he does.

AJ is dreaming again. He's hoping for a better future with a sense of empowerment that he can make it happen. He is making his own path out of his rut and into a life that is meaningful for him.

Key Takeaways

- To stop the old habits that are holding you back, you need to have new habits that will propel you forward.
- The 20-Second Rule and Pomodoro Technique are great ways to keep you on track for your new habits to take shape and get things done.
- Imagine a future where you are living according to your definition of success and achieving goals that resonate with your sense of purpose. Share with me what that looks like at info@beyondtherut.com, and put "My life Beyond the Rut" in the Subject line.

PART IV

Our Stories Matter, So Tell Your Story and Change the World

"No matter what people tell you, words and ideas can change the world." – Robin Williams

CHAPTER 11

My Beyond the Rut Story

I was born into a military family. My dad was a military policeman in the U.S. Army. He was married to a woman he met while stationed in Thailand during the Vietnam War. Life was good overall. I got to live in countries like Germany and Japan and visit Thailand and Korea while growing up. Not many of my friends today can say they had that kind of education when they were kids.

My mom was the stereotypical Tiger Mom. She expected me to not only get good grades but I had to be the top performer in my class all the time in everything. That builds a certain level of arrogance in someone, I believe, and it's a miracle I had friends at all. The silver lining, I suppose, was the desire to do well in anything I took on.

There was also the darker side of life while growing up that many people would not know just by looking at me today. My parents divorced when I was 11 years old. That drove my dad towards attempting suicide. It was not the life we expected. My dad had been restationed to Germany, and my brother and I went with him while my mom stayed in California. That first night in our own apartment was when my dad held a butcher's knife to his chest, mustering the courage to drive it in. My brother was nine years old at the time. All of us were crying. My brother and I screamed at my dad to put the knife down, and he did.

That started our crash course in suicide prevention for my brother and me. We were kids. What did we know? We wanted to be kids. Instead, we kept this secret to ourselves. My dad's work couldn't know. They might kick him out of the Army. My mom couldn't know because she'd try to take over custody and who knows what her new boyfriend would do.

My little brother and I put every sharp object into a plastic bucket and hid that bucket in the basement of our apartment building. We monitored my dad's prescription medication to make sure he did not attempt to overdose on them. We timed how long it took to drive from our apartment to his office and called his work to make sure he arrived on time and called again in the evenings to make sure he was starting his trip home. Any deviation and we threatened to tell his boss.

One summer day, however, he managed to hang himself. There was no way that an 11-year-old boy barely four and a half feet tall could hold up a grown man around 175 pounds. The lanyard cord he used to hang himself held up very well, and we had no knives in the home thanks to our reaction to that first night in our home. I'm grateful to this day that the little clip on that lanyard was not rated for that kind of weight, and it snapped, dropping my dad to the floor.

My dad lived. We cried through it all, and he promised he would not try that ever again. He regretted it as he passed out hanging from the closet door. Another blessing in disguise was that the lanyard left a mark on his neck that he could not hide. His boss saw it the next day in the office and immediately ordered my dad to get psychiatric care. My brother and I were placed with a foster family while he was in an Army hospital in Germany, getting the professional help and support he needed.

The family we were placed with was great. They actually ate their meals together, talked through their conflicts in a civil way, and demonstrated love for each other and their neighbors. The experience was counter to everything I had ever experienced growing up so far and what I would experience for the rest of my school days. A new paradigm had been introduced to me.

A First Line in the Sand

I wish I could tell you that things were all better after that, but there were more years of "growing" left ahead. My dad was restationed back to California, where he could be closer to his family for support. Our weekend trips to the Bay Area meant my dad could talk with his parents and siblings and feel normal and validated again. His care and counseling also continued for many more years.

The problem was that many of these family members were also growing through their own problems, like divorce, and had little to offer in terms of emotional support. Hurt people hurt people, after all. My memories of going to my grandparents' house meant many days of boredom, hopelessness, and being bullied by a cousin, his best friend, and even an uncle of mine.

While my dad was getting the support he needed, I was getting pummeled behind his back. Family flung names at me like Gook, Chink, Nip, Half-breed, and more. It felt like I survived one hell only to go through another one. This time it was the very people who should have shown me more kindness. That continued for three more years until my dad finally saw what was happening and believed me. It was the last time I had to go up to my grandparents with him if I didn't want to go, and I began to limit my interactions with them.

Many of the people in my extended family were nice, though, and I did not want to see them go through life without hope, either. At 14 years old, I gave everyone at Christmas a personal card or note from me that shared my line in the sand moment with them. I wanted to live up to the Dugan crest's motto, "By Virtue and Valor." I wanted to be the first in the family to graduate from a university with a degree. I wanted to show everyone that it was possible to create the life we want to live rather than resign to living off welfare for the rest of our lives. In a way, it was my first written goal.

For some in my family, it became a point of inspiration, and some cousins still remember that note and even hold onto it. For others, it did not go well at all. It seems there is always going to be someone close to you who will be scared or jealous of your desire to have a better life than you had yesterday because you represent what they are not doing for themselves.

High school went very well for me. I played football for four years, baseball for three, and played tuba in the band all four years as well. I was recruited to University of the Pacific for tuba performance, although I pulled a switcheroo and went with a pre-med program instead. I still played in the band and the Pacific Pep Band (mostly for the stipend and free hot dog and soda). I barely graduated with a Bachelor of Science in Chemistry-Biology, and that's BARELY in all capital letters.

If I wanted to be a physician, I would need more than a dismal 2.1 grade point average. I was also broke and used up all my available financial aid. That led me to join the U.S. Army as a medic to gain experience, utilize the G.I. Bill, and travel the world on the government's dime. After a deployment to Kosovo in 2000, I met a fellow soldier named Olivia. We started dating, got married, and built a family together. My Army career ended in 2003 after a deployment with the 3rd Infantry Division to invade Iraq.

The three biggest takeaways for me from Operation Iraqi Freedom were that I loved my family very much, I hated seeing the phrase "we're taking care of your family for you" in the letters of support that came to me, and that war robs the world of its youth and talent. I had decided after that tour that life was just too short to tempt Death every time I suited up for work. Even if I survived a career in the Army, the medals and promotions from all the deployments that would come were not worth missing my children growing up and becoming a total stranger to my wife.

I left the Army in 2003 and started my first civilian career as an Education Coordinator running the orientation program for new employees in a healthcare system because it was the best way to leverage my education, my leadership skills, and training experience from the Army into a paycheck that would support my family. It was also when I realized that after four years in a pre-med program and four years in the U.S. Army as a medic, I did not want to become a nurse or a doctor. Those professions were someone else's dream for me and not my own. That's when I hit my first rut.

My First Rut

I remember lying in bed the day after Christmas in 2005. We had just spent the entire year sacrificing to pay off credit card debt. That victory was overshadowed by the reality that we had used that same credit card to buy Christmas presents. Rather than being on a path toward financial freedom, our family was back in the hole where we started a year ago.

My two-week vacation felt more like a furlough from a prison sentence, and I was about to go back into my cell. The job I loved felt like an obligation now. The pattern was clear, and it was grim. I was officially in the rat race, an exhausting and unfulfilling attempt to chase success, only to find myself in a vicious cycle. The rat race tempts with promotions and pay raises. Credit gets extended because of the higher salary, and we accepted that credit. Our spending increased with every pay raise and tax return boost. We had a sense of what we thought was "the good life."

This downward spiral went unchecked, and now I was lying in bed the day after Christmas realizing that I was trapped in debt. Our annual family trips were now for places like "Maybe Next Year" and "Not Right Now." That was just on the money side.

I read a book called *Rich Dad Poor Dad* by Robert Kiyosaki and learned that owning businesses was the best way to build wealth. It was clear I needed to learn more about business. At the same time, I was now reporting to a new boss, and her insecurity appeared practically on Day 1. She let go of five people in just three months, and I was the fifth person. It was demoralizing when she told me, "I'm putting together a team of go-getters, and you are not that." It was a slap to the face since I was anything but a slacker.

The next five years were a challenge. I dove into being a real estate sales agent and was doing well the first two years before the real estate bubble burst in 2007. Stubbornly, I stayed in real estate until the end of 2010 and finally took a job as a Community Educator for a battered women's shelter. I had accepted that my zone of genius was in training and educating others, and I was happiest and performed best in training and speaking roles. Not only did this new job put me on a path that was better aligned with my skills, strengths, and passion, but it also saved our home from foreclosure.

We don't have to be like everyone else!

It wasn't all bad, either. Being self-employed allowed me to volunteer at my children's schools. I plugged in with a men's ministry and attended Bible studies, which helped sharpen my faith and gave me a support network when things were not going well. Financially, it was a dead end for us, though. We were always one commission check too short.

Going through this experience reminded me that I didn't want to be like everyone else. I had never been like everyone else. Being normal was being part of the 93% of Americans with so much consumer debt that they have a negative net worth. Being normal meant not being able to retire comfortably. It meant trading my life for paying bills on things that ultimately didn't matter. Being normal meant fewer travel experiences.

Finding My Groove Again

Taking on that job with the women's shelter was a blessing. Training and development turned out to be my sweet spot. I used the G.I. Bill to pick up a Master's Degree in Educational Technology, which had a focus on instructional design. That led to a job that doubled my income and my first promotion into a leadership role outside of the Army. My income doubled again when I was hired to be a director of a learning and development team.

I took up podcasting in 2013 as a way to express my ministry to other men about living an authentic life. My dream has been to become an author, speaker, and educator who helps men get out of living a caricature life so they can be genuine, humble servant leaders in their families and communities. That's what led to my first podcast called Family Time Q&A, which was about my family asking me anything they wanted, and I would have to answer without a script and without editing the interview. My hope was that I would demonstrate the results of servant leadership in the home.

The show never became a viral sensation, but those who listened shared that it encouraged them to be the best husbands and fathers they could be. It also led to a friend of mine recruiting me to help him start a podcast. He wanted a show that would encourage and equip men to live their lives following biblical principles and in the context of Jesus Christ. The twist was that we wanted the Jesus part to be there without really thumping listeners with Bible verses or condemnation. That's how Beyond the Rut launched its first episode on August 15, 2015.

At the time of this writing, Beyond the Rut has roughly 3,000 listeners, according to Rephonic, and ranks globally among the top 2.5% according to ListenNotes.

My Second Rut and Beyond

I took a job in late 2019 that would promote me to a director-level corporate role and come with a serious pay increase. The job represented a quadrupling of my income from my days as a community educator and would pave the way for my wife and me to enjoy our empty nesting years. Taking that job was an opportunity, and it came at a price.

My daughter was promised that she would be able to finish high school where she was, and I wasn't one to break promises. The finances were right, and Olivia (my wife) and I agreed that I would get an apartment in Dallas and commute between Dallas and Corpus Christi for the next year and a half until Emma graduated. I knew the moment I landed in Dallas and had my first meeting with my new boss that I had made a mistake. I was already feeling trapped in my new arrangement.

We decided to give it a few months, and I was about to call it quits when the COVID-19 pandemic broke out. We were on lockdown for a month, and my team and organization needed my skills, so there wasn't much to do but hunker down. Companies around the world would later put employees on furlough and then eventually layoffs to stay afloat. I had a full-time job paying very well. Things weren't as bad as they could be.

A new project kicked off, and that offered a great feather in my cap. The paycheck got bigger, and the bonuses were nice. It was all costing me as much as it was covering what my family needed. While I was home for the majority of my daughter's high school milestones, I missed out on the day-to-day life before she graduated. My wife was tempted to stay in Corpus Christi to be close to her. It only made sense to hang it up where I was whether or not the project was complete. We decided to see the project through, at least.

The big project launched, and the impact of the Great Resignation kicked in. I was losing my team for a variety of reasons, but through it all, I realized I was in another rut. Despite some great projects, I felt like I was not really growing or making an impact where I was. Beyond the Rut was hitting a stagnation that could end the life of the podcast. I was giving up on a life with impact for a steady and generous paycheck. That flew in the face of what Beyond the Rut is about.

The very thing I was helping people recognize and build a path beyond that rut was where I found myself. I was checking off the boxes of success, but it was becoming clear they weren't my own boxes. My own dreams were going on the back burner as a "side gig." The stress of the job was coming home with me and putting a strain on my marriage and my health. My wife and my friends all noticed this shift and often asked me, "Why don't you just quit?"

So, I left my full-time job to finish this book, launch it, launch a business, and decide after a few months what's next. I'm excited about it because we're financially in a good place to take a few months to work through this. I've been developing myself through podcasting and a daily routine of positive habits to prepare for this transition. Now is the time. As you create your own path beyond your rut, I'm also doing the same thing as you read this book!

The point here is that if you're not careful, that groove you create can become a new rut. Keep making your own path out of that rut, and be a comfort zone killer.

CHAPTER 12

Tell Your Story to Pay It Forward

At this point, you have realized that you're living in a rut in some part of your life. You looked up, and you looked forward. You've begun to design the life you want to live, and you've drawn that line in the sand to take the first step on your new path. As you live your new journey, you need to tell your story. You need to tell your story because there are others out there like you who are stuck in a rut. Your story can be the wake-up call someone needs to hear today, whether they act on it or not. Your story may be the very thing that gives somebody the moment needed to realize their own rut, and they begin to design a life of their own as well.

It is not arrogance to share your story. It could be done in a way that is vulnerable and honest. That is what people are drawn to—the reality of what is. They don't want some person with a cookie cutter perfect-looking lifestyle. Yes, that draws people on Instagram. When it comes to actually seeing that something can be done, knowing your story and your struggles makes it even more real.

Sharing your story takes courage. It takes courage because you are opening yourself up. There are going to be people out there who are like drowning victims. They're desperately clamoring for life and freedom but will inadvertently attempt to drown anyone who comes along who is moving up or trying to help them. Understand that hurt people hurt people. Insecure people will resist you and even attack your intentions because your journey reminds them of how stuck they really are. Do not let their insecurities and fear be the reason why you hold yourself back.

You are on a new path. For every "hater" you encounter, there will be many others who will be inspired and equipped by what you experienced and the transformation you created in your life.

How will you share your story?

Why Beyond the Rut Exists

Beyond the Rut began as a collaboration among three friends who served together in a Christian Men's Ministry. My friend, Brandon, invited me and another friend named Shawn to discuss his desire to start a podcast. Brandon, serving as an associate pastor at a local church, shared how many Christian men struggled with the same questions every weekend related to careers, finances, marriage, and being a father. They would share how they felt overall that their lives were at a dead end and stuck in a rut.

It was having these discussions every single week over and over and over that made Brandon think, "What if I could capture these answers and just have them ready for play-back?" It was often the same men asking the same exact ques-tion, clearly not making any change whatsoever. Maybe, just maybe, the recorded version could help someone else, even if it wasn't the original audience for that advice. A recorded message could be played repeatedly until it was understood. Zig Ziglar, salesman and public speaker, said that it takes at least seven times for somebody to hear something for it to finally stick.

Beyond the Rut is about helping you break the patterns that have you stuck in a rut so that you can live a fulfilled, meaningful life that makes an impact on yourself, your family, and your community. You are uniquely and wonder-fully created. I believe that you have a purpose to fulfill.

Life is not without struggle or without difficulty. Life is filled with both. Just like the end of every hike I've accom-plished, the view at the top of the summit and the feeling of accomplishment are worth it. You get to be a part of that world. You get to look up and see everything that's around. You look forward to see the impact you want your life to have, and then you can take action to make it so. Beyond the Rut is here to encourage you, inspire you, and equip you with practical tips to make your dream a reality without com-promising your faith or your family or your career.

Join Rutter Nation

You do not have to take this journey alone. Rutter Nation is a community growing that is filled with people also pursuing their own paths to get out of their own ruts. This community is coming together to synergize, share stories, and be inspired to grow into something new. Anyone and everyone seeking to live life beyond their own rut are Rutters, and they can inspire other people to become a part of Rutter Nation.

Bookmark the Beyond the Rut website on your web browsers, BeyondTheRut.com. Follow @beyondtherut on social media, and join the Rutter Nation weekly newsletter, where I share more stories and practical tools to help you create the life you want to live beyond the rut, BeyondTheRut. com/email.

It's my belief that as we have more connections, we make a big world small. We can grow from each other and, in return, make the world around us a better place. Thank you for taking the time to read this book. I invite you to accept one of our invitations to our connection points listed below and go live life beyond the rut.

NOTES

[1] 2022 Credit Card Debt Statistics, https://www.lendingtree.com/credit-cards/credit-card-debt-statistics/

[2] Matthews, Gail. (2007) "The Impact of Commitment, Accountability, and Written Goals on Goal Achievement." Psychology | Faculty Presentations. 3. https://scholar.dominican.edu/psychology-faculty-conference-presentations/3

[3] http://www.irishgenealogy.com/biography/kitty/dugan.htm

RESOURCES

You can find me on the web at www.BeyondTheRut.com or connect on LinkedIn at www.linkedin.com/in/jerrydugan. My goal is to help you make the most out of this life in the areas of your faith, family, fitness, finances, and future possibility. Below are the resources mentioned throughout this book plus a few extras. Go live life Beyond the Rut!

The FREE Audiobook, www.beyondtherut.com/audiobook
Measure It to Make It, www.beyondtherut.com/goals
Getting Out of Your Rut Journal, www.beyondtherut.com/getout
10 Questions to Identify Your Limiting Beliefs, www.beyondtherut.com/limitingbeliefs
Beyond the Rut podcast, www.beyondtherut.com/podcast-2
BtR Impact, LLC, building servant leaders through coaching, consulting, training workshops, and keynotes, www.btrimpact.com

AUTHOR BIO

 Jerry Dugan is a leadership consultant, training facilitator, and public speaker who hosts the podcast Beyond the Rut. He helps build servant leaders by finding clarity and alignment in their work and personal lives.

His leadership experience includes roles with the U.S. Army, Christian ministry, and corporate healthcare where his whole-person approach has built thriving teams who found joy in their work as part of their lives. His personal belief that life is too short to live stuck in a rut drives his hope to help you create success that doesn't cost you your faith or your family.

BtR 🎤 IMPACT LLC

WORK WITH ME!

Helping servant leaders define success and improve interpersonal dynamics so they can create meaningful work and impactful teams while also thriving in their faith, their family, and their health.

Keynote Speaking
Team-Building Workshops
Leadership Development Workshops
Coaching & Consulting

BTRIMPACT.COM

URGENT REQUEST

Thank you for reading my book
and committing to living a life beyond the rut!
I'd appreciate your feedback to make the next version
of this book and future books better.

Please take two minutes right now to leave a helpful review
on Amazon and let me know what you thought
about this book.

Go to beyondtherut.com/bookreview.

Thanks so much!

Jerry Dugan

Self-Publishing
School

NOW IT'S YOUR TURN

Discover the EXACT 3-step blueprint you need to become a bestselling author in as little as 3 months.

Self-Publishing School helped me, and now I want them to help you with this FREE resource to begin outlining your book!

Even if you're busy, bad at writing, or don't know where to start, you CAN write a bestseller and build your best life.

With tools and experience across a variety of niches and professions, Self-Publishing School is the only resource you need to take your book to the finish line!

DON'T WAIT

Say "YES" to becoming a bestseller:

www.self-publishingschool.com/friend/

Follow the steps on the page to get a FREE resource to get started on your book and unlock a discount to get started with Self-Publishing School.

Made in the USA
Coppell, TX
18 April 2023

15750925R00069